My Baby Sister N

By Sharon Rose Anderson
Illustrated by Randy Haws

©2015 Sharon Rose Anderson

Illustrated by Randy Haws.

Printed and bound in the United States of America. All rights reserved. No part of this book may be reproduced or transmitted in any form or by any means, electronic or mechanical, including photocopying, recording, or by an information storage and retrieval system—except by a review who may quote brief passages and in a review to be printed in a magazine, newspaper, or by the Web—without permission in writing from the publisher.

ORDERING INFORMATION:

Additional copies of **My Baby Sister Needs Me** are available online at:

www.amazon.com

First printing 2015

ISBN-13: 978-1514278796 and ISBN-10: 1514278790

DEDICATION

This book is dedicated to my four precious granddaughters who inspire me everyday. I love you forever and for always.

Something's different about my family, something strange.
I have a feeling some things are going to change.

It was just Mommy, Daddy, and me before.
Now it seems we'll be a family of four!

Oh, how things have changed, I was right.
I have become a big sister overnight.

I'm not sure what a big sister should do.
I'll have to ask Mommy, Daddy, and others, too.

Mommy said my baby sister needs me,
and there's so much to be done.
Getting diapers, binkies and toys,
oh, the fun has just begun.

8

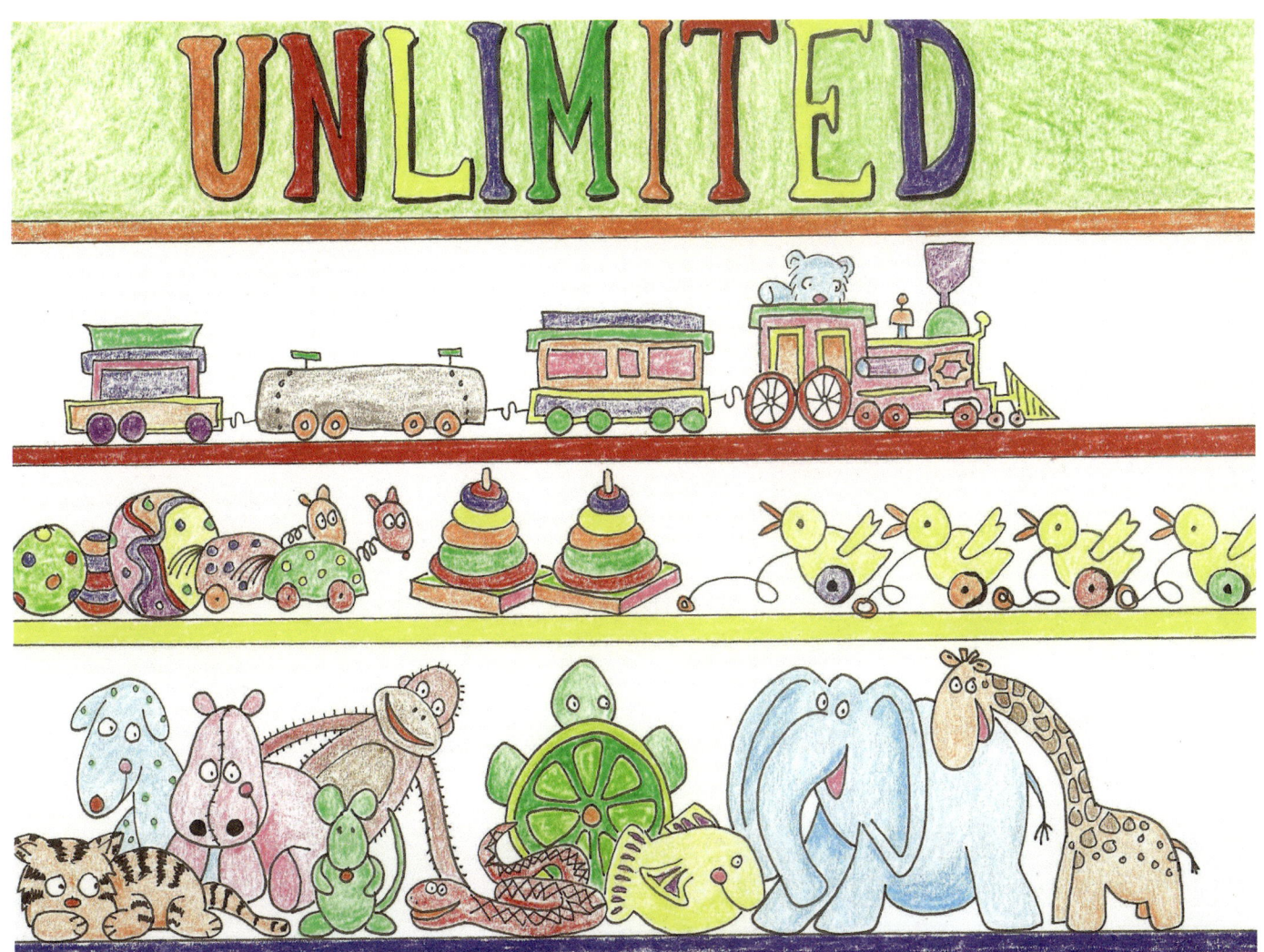

Daddy said getting her a special gift
just from me would be fun.
With my daddy's help, I will find the very best one.

Grandma said I should read lots of books
to make her smile.
I'll pick out my favorites and read the whole pile.

Grandpa said I should find ways to make her giggle.
I'll gently tickle her,
then watch her laugh and wiggle.

My cousin said I should teach her how to splish and splash.
Then we can have lots of fun when taking a bath.

My teacher said I need to be soft and gentle, too.
That's because my baby sister is so little and new.

My aunt said I should pick out
nice clothes for her to wear.
I'll find the best outfits ever,
just to show her I care.

My uncle said I should sing until she falls asleep.
I sure hope she sleeps all night without a peep.

People have suggested lots of helpful things I can do.

I am excited to help my baby sister with my own ideas, too.

When she's big enough, I can push her in a swing.
Teaching her to hold on tight
is a very important thing.

I'll teach her to find
a safe waiting spot
for putting our feet.
Then we can look for cars
before crossing any street.

I like being a big sister,
and I'll be the best I can be.

I am proud and happy to say,
"That's MY baby sister, and she needs me."

THE END

Printed in Great Britain
by Amazon